THEY SPEAK OF FRUIT

Gary L. McDowell

Cooper
Dillon

Cooper Dillon Books
San Diego, California
www.CooperDillon.com

Cover art: Eric Person
Cover Design: Max Xiantu
Layout: remixt
ISBN: 978-0-9841928-0-9

Acknowledgements:
Grateful acknowledgement is made to the following journals where
these poems first appeared or are forthcoming, though some in dif-
ferent forms:

Anti–: "How Mosquitoes Came to Be"
Bat City Review: "All Stones Are Broken Stones"
Bateau: "Diary of a Carpenter Wasp" and "Diary of a Horsefly"
Copper Nickel: "Tumbling Woman"
Memorious: "Nectar"
New England Review: "Ninth Morning in a Row with Binoculars"
No Tell Motel: "Yellow Jackets" and "Flesh" (as "Bones Hurt When
They Have Flesh on Them")
Parthenon West Review: "Blackbirds"

"Ninth Morning in a Row with Binoculars" was featured on
Poetry Daily on October 2, 2008.

TABLE OF CONTENTS

No wonder of it: shéer plód makes plough down sillion
Shine, and blue-bleak embers, ah my dear,
Fall, gall themselves, and gash gold-vermillion.

—Gerard Manley Hopkins

ALL STONES ARE BROKEN STONES

Last night I dreamt of swallows
flying from her mouth:
their slanted wings left cuts in her throat.

She looked content with their expulsion,
her flesh eager and moist.
A bustle of blue backs thrusting:
the gathering of twigs and stones,
and gravity resolved in her ribcage.

They speak of fruit.
Their tail streamers scissor the fervent thread
and drink her of her ashen body—

NECTAR

I found my history in the tiny
bones of a hummingbird, its beating heart
that could fill a thimble with its blood.
Its subtle feet and soft beak,
never again to fly sideways
or beat its wings faster
than a prayer can leave.

And for that, I offer a prayer:
hummingbird, fly into my mouth and lay
your head under my tongue.
Let me turn your death
against my teeth
and weigh it, and weigh myself.

I sing the days in the morning. My breath weighs less than a chickadee's. Voice is a good detractor. So are wings. I have learned a few things and studied many. Mostly things change. Angles and feathers. It's always about birds. Flying and not. That they sing at all makes me aware of their lightness, their eruptive, hollow chutes that when palmed look exactly like the living do. I should breathe and relax. But like pilgrims, I am a fool gone too far.

BLACKBIRDS

1

I've never seen him without a beard,
                        but the sputtering light of the fire,
the shadows, help me imagine
how he looks clean-shaven.

        Pine logs settle and burn, snapping
                                at the bottom of the fire pit.
Heat on my forehead; the hair on my knuckles

stands up, pulled straight by heat,
                        so close to my hands.

The breeze swirls around the fire, throwing bright ash
in our laps.

Above us, night has spread;

                                the star's vibrance
this far from the city.

        My father holds a rifle in his lap, polished
and unused for over ten years; we are quiet.

Where have we been and how is it we've never lost our way?

/
Another log burns in the fire,
                    and still I wish I could've grown a beard,
or even a passable shadow

        to hide my sweat
as we cleared Grandfather's house of his belongings,
kept only what he loved:

a circular saw, pictures of my grandmother,
a few crappies mounted on plaques, and his rifle.

        My father didn't sweat at all,
                    didn't speak on the drive home,
only nodded his head to the radio.

The fire is dimming now, and my father points
the rifle to the sky, spies through the sights,
                    that there is Ursa Minor
and over there, he swings to the left and points
                        South and low over the horizon,
is Scorpius.

/
My grandfather: *stay away from the purple crows.*
                    Their iridescent wings, black beaks
and feet like cowhide only blacker, and how they'd mimic
        the cocking of our rifles, our laughs,

and the nightly applause for Johnny Carson.

My father: *Crows—too quick to shoo away, too illegal to shoot.*

It was at our cabin in Arbor Vitae, Wisconsin
where my father and grandfather would sit for hours
                              watching blackbirds,

where I'd put my father's rifle to my shoulder
lean my head against the butt stock,

                              caw-caw

and my father, the graceful way he'd pull
                              the rifle from my hands
and tell me *blackbirds, son. Shoot only the blackbirds.*

There's enough of those to go around
                              and you wouldn't want to upset
your grandfather.

/
              My grandfather a boy, the rifle strapped to his shoulder,
the leather rough and hot.
A brown satchel on his other shoulder,

and later, fifteen years later,
                              he'd show my father how to hold
a rifle steady against his cheek,
show him the right way to stoke a fire on the lake shore,
              show him, when at the cabin, how to call home
                              every third day,
to check-in with Grandma.

My father a boy, following his father into the woods.
The undergrowth along the backyard fence is burnt
just enough they can hurdle it
                              and walk easily into the forest,

tracking with their cocker a flush of pheasants.
                              And when they're distracted

by a brace of blackbirds,
does my grandfather know to hand his son the rifle
                              because it will be an easy first shot

or because he remembers the smell
of gunpowder and pond water, hot leather against his skin?

And years later I'd read of the red-winged blackbirds,
                              their scarlet shoulder patches,
their pinkish chin
and throat.

Their call from the stumps of dead oaks:
                              an inhaled whistle,
a breath not quite fulfilled
like a man casting and casting his bait into the lake—

DIARY OF A HORSEFLY

Until bones, your bones, fall to the ground, I'll not show myself. Only the rustling of my wings like cattails gives me away. My body is the badlands and I am lost. My flesh is not your flesh. I will not let my eyes turn for you. I am made of valleys, and I too have needs. I want breadth. I want breadth around me and within me. I want you to admit you are a hill. You are rock. Given enough time to starve, any man will chase a rabbit until he dies from exhaustion. He hopes for only one bite of the fibrous meat, one slurp of the hot, slain blood.

TUMBLING WOMAN

SIDE VIEW

She was only four minutes into her act when the black-winged flying fish leapt from the sea. Its pelvic fins spread out like wings, so eerily calm in the air, its body motionless. It was a brief flight. The ringleader mistook the fish for her. In his haste he proclaimed her alive while she was still under the great undulating waves, still riding the current. She was free to drown. And if she blacked out upon surfacing, the crowd would roar even louder. She needed to hold her breath until her pastry lungs leaked acid into her blood, until the veins in her forehead throbbed like mountain slopes. It was her job to drown. Intentionally and violently. And the people would rejoice. It was her job to drown. But she could not drink enough water to do it herself. She needed gills to think about the possibilities.

In the beginning, she chose her act in good faith but since has grown more bitter with the salt of the continents. First she fed their appetite for pathos and used a bathtub. The upwelling of water from the basin's bottom carried with it applause and small cones of light only visible through her clenched eyewalls. But that wasn't enough. The stage wasn't grand enough. So when Earth's most ancient rocks had bled enough to form the salty sea, which was young when the earth was young, she, naked and cold, fed herself to the currents. As she sank, she felt at home descending past colonies of sharp-jawed arrowworms, those fierce, half-inch long dragons. Then gooseberrylike comb jellies whose stings contained hints of the history of the sun. And neither was she surprised when she stopped sinking in a thick cloud of krill, their nearly invisible bristling appendages straining plankton from the water. Self-drowning had once been haled as the next worm-eating. But when the moon was born there was no ocean, only soil. She wandered just long enough. She always rose exactly five minutes and twenty-three seconds after her descent. At five minutes, the ringleader pronounced her dead. Those extra twenty-three seconds made the audience think she'd been crushed by the great sinking masses of surface water. They mumbled that the deep and turbulent vast rivers of ocean had swept her away. And on land, ghost crabs continued to speed along the beaches, dashing periodically into the surf to moisten their gills before hiding again in their small, burrowed-out homes. Necessities are few but wants are endless. Her boiling blonde hair would break the surface in time with the audience's gasps. In some small way, she wanted to drown, wanted to give them the long, slow death by way of sea they had hoped for. But her act was perfect the way it was. Unfinished and asinine.

MAQUETTE

She modeled her act after the glassworm and the winged snail. Or maybe, probably, after the sea slug—a snail without a shell. That soft, shapeless brown flesh patterned with night-edged circles and fringed with flaps and folds of skin. How she crept over the sargassum weeds mimicking the branching fronds, the golden berries, and even the white dots of encrusted worm tubes. How she felt at home. The sea was her meat. The sea was her cradle, her knapsack of stars. She ached to be fierce. She ached to be acknowledged. She ached as though her spine were unzipped. She ached to be other.

Yellow Jackets

for Amy Newman

I've come to see the Queen's chamber,
                              the layers of honey
and paper-mâché surroundings

her head bowed, her supple body as others serve her—
        so I can tell her that I am

what I seem, but the hive is jumping
and there is no language to convince her.

        I wait and watch for a change in the light
or the heat or my want and one

                by one from the hive they come,

the swift curve of their stingers,
and the shadow of their humid wings,

                their eyes like carnival mirrors,
as we rise off the roof into
a hard new language.

The Whole Of It

/
I could tell you.

How the blue-winged teal scuttles
over the grass
and regains the water.

How the pond outside my window,
gated and fenced,
(no kids will drown there)
in prairie-pothole-country,
is not a marsh, not a wetland, not a grassland,

or a flooded ditch
on a golf course.

But a shallow pond. And when frightened, the teal
springs directly into flight,
never patters on the water while getting airborne.

What am I
tethered? What am I divorced?

/
So much to wish.

A poem about watching a teal, about my grandmother,

about the experience of watching a teal

fly to the middle of the pond, her mottled gray-brown
body plumage,
her pale head,
her blue upper wings, (she's a she

because there's no white crescent on her face,
no white on her underwing)

a poem about nature's most efficient machines:

birds and how they move, a poem
about missing you.

So much I wish I could tell you.

How I am lost in the city-of-best-words,
the imagination's particulars.

(This is good. To purge.)

The idea-man,
the man-the-boy-who-jars-his-city

only to open it later when it's raining.

I own thousands of envelopes.

I should have written you more letters.

What is solid? *What* is rather dull.

I will mail you
            a poem about
the teal and her diet.

/
The blue-wings are the first ducks south in the fall
            and the last north in the spring:

they have it right: go to the middle of a pond

                        and sleep by night
under the moon, their bills tucked and nestled into their
            feathers.
                        And that moon,
its trumpet-horn, subscribes to the engine: the what that
keeps us
            from flying.

                  What is confirmed? Lost?

(Blue wings and black patches. Get this, teals eat duckweed.

Or mollusks and insects. Small seeds of aquatic plants.
            Their bills
                        so thin).

            And they utter a cricketlike call. Do you remember
hearing that call in the early mornings? Out the window
                        over your pond
not unlike my pond. How the drake would wait patiently,

his brown speckled breast, his blackish crown,

and your coffee thinned with cream,
the sun off the water, your hummingbird feeder swinging

                                        in the garden.

The smallest of all the dabbling ducks.

She was so.

/
Time, it seems to me, doesn't fly,

it's more the-halls-of-all-the-pretty-things that fly,
        leave us earliest in the morning

                                        without a bird
to watch, without a window to call our own,

but I am the idea-man

        (there's so many idea-men)

                        and I am the-boy-who-lost-
himself watching that blue-winged teal
                circle the pond,

and all that's left in her wake is the water.

I'm in my truck, I-94, I-80—they're all the same—
when a spring-robin flies into my cabin, knocks
off the rearview mirror and falls onto the passenger

seat, shocked, out cold, its caramel feet docile
against its chest. I, too, am breathless, unsure
whether to pull over or throw the robin out

the window before it wakes. How does one
resuscitate a bird? How does one know when
to resuscitate a bird? Two nights ago the weatherman

said *spring is finally here,* said *fire up those grills, folks,
it's bratwurst time!* What an odd thing to say.
Every morning a cardinal whistles from the heavy

pine outside my bedroom, his trills enough
to stir my dogs who know now the sun has risen.
I sip coffee on the porch and watch the cardinal

tease his mate, his black face, his crest, how he shares
seeds by kissing her beak: he perches on a fence post,
harmonizes with her, phrases with her: their banter.

Behind the house, cars race by on US-131, the whoosh
of semis, their long haul beginning or nearly ending,
and I remember baseball scores from the radio

the night before: *Chicago dismantles Houston, 9-3,*
and the Pirates blow a late lead, fall 8-6 to the Fins. So final.
The everyday becomes more everyday every day,

yet still I wish I could cup that robin
in my palms and breathe life back into him, but this spring
is its last, and lying on my passenger seat is the face

I fear most, the face I've never touched but that I must
touch to make authentic, to make other than silent.
It's asking too much to bring back the fallen:

our hands are busy enough predicting the weather,
busy enough flipping through radio stations to find
the ballgame, to find a voice that'll tell us *good pitching*

will beat good hitting any time, and vice versa.

How Mosquitos Came To Be

for Mildred Huyck

She followed the giant for so long that she thought she was his blood, his hair, his lactose eyes. *You cannot kill him with a knife,* they warned her.

She possumed in front of the giant's cave until he took her in. She thrust her knife into his left heel, where he kept his heart. Tough and gristly, the years of callous. She felt his heartbeat dying in the handle of the knife.

I will feast on human flesh until time dies, he cried. *You cannot kill me.*

She stoked a fire and cut him into pieces then threw his ashes into the wind to scatter. Each particle refused to touch ground and sprung wings instead. Busy wings. And bloodened wings. Long legs and compound eyes. Flight muscles. Serrated mouths and proteinic saliva.

She felt a sting on her cheek, her arm, her neck. She made heat with her fingernails. She wished she could be wingéd and small as ash.

FLESH

Falls come suddenly. A kestrel's body
language, the flipping of a wing
that mimics a branch in the breeze.
But who mourns the loss of a mouse,
of a shrew? Sometimes an empty field
becomes beautiful in the escaping light
of evening. In hauntingly small lives
we assemble this loop, this curl, where
all flesh is not alike, where all shadows
mistrust the darkness, and all bodies will rise
whether in a mouth or in heat
up into the patch of night-time
on a hill, or the mirrors in the trees
that help the kestrel hunt, or into an hour
of parody where we arrange God.

Cooper
Dillon

ISBN 978-0-9841928-0-9

90000

9 780984 192809

ISBN: 978-0-9841928-0-9